WEIRD

AND

WONDERFUL

FROGS &TOADS

HELEN RILEY

Thomson Learning
New York

WEIRD AND WONDERFUL

FISH
FROGS & TOADS
INSECTS
SNAKES

Cover: A red-eyed leaf frog from Costa Rica.

First published in the United States in 1993 by
Thomson Learning, 115 Fifth Avenue, New York, NY 10003

First published in the United Kingdom in 1991 by
Wayland (Publishers) Ltd.

Library of Congress Cataloging-in-Publication Data

Riley, Helen.
  Frogs & toads / Helen Riley.
      p.   cm. — (Weird and wonderful)
  "First published in 1991 by Wayland (Publishers) …
Hove, East Sussex, England" — T.p. verso.
  Includes bibliographical references (p.) and index.
  Summary: Describes the characteristics of several species
of frogs and toads considered unique and distinctive because
of their physiology, habits, and habitats.
  ISBN 1-56847-007-X (hardcover)
  ISBN 1-56847-302-8 (paperback)
   1. Frogs—Juvenile literature. 2. Toads—Juvenile literature.
[1. Frogs. 2. Toads.] I. Title. II. Title: Frogs and toads.
III. Series.
QL668.E2R55   1993
597.8 — dc20   92-41476

Printed in the United States of America

CONTENTS

1. Different sizes

Compared to many other **vertebrates,** frogs and toads are all on the small side. Like all **amphibians,** frogs and toads are cold-blooded animals. That means that the temperature of their bodies does not remain constant but changes as the temperature of their surroundings changes. Frogs and toads rely on heat from their surroundings to warm themselves; it is better to be small because a small body takes less time to warm up.

The biggest **species** of frog is the goliath frog, which lives in the rain forests of West Africa. This shy creature can measure up to 12 inches (30 cm) from snout to **vent,** and more than twice that with its back legs outstretched. Goliath frogs live in deep pools in rivers in the African forests. As the goliath frog is so big, local people often hunt it for food. They believe that this frog's leg bones have magical powers to bring good luck.

One of the smallest species of frog or toad is the pygmy golden frog from Brazil. It measure less than 1 inch (2.5 cm) in length. This tiny frog lives among the dead leaves on the floor of the forest. Still other species are even smaller, only ½ inch (1.3 cm) long.

Below The goliath frog is the world's largest frog.

Right A pygmy golden frog from the rain forests of Brazil.

2. Strange shapes

Some species of frogs and toads have very strange shapes. Although they may look very odd, their bodies have adapted (changed) for a special reason.

The spatulate nosed tree frog from Central America has a long nose with wide flattened end, a bit like a spoon. It uses its nose to lift up sections of the bark of trees. The frog then crawls into the hole it has made and uses the end of its nose to block up the entrance. Sealed safely inside its hole, the spatulate nosed tree frog is safe from **predators**.

Most frogs and toads live on land as well as in water and so they breathe air through their **lungs**.

The Lake Titicaca frog spends all of its life underwater, so its body has adapted in a very unusual way. Unlike most other frogs and toads it has no lungs. Instead, it breathes through its skin. The Lake Titicaca frog has large folds of skin that drape from the sides of its body. These extra folds increase the surface area of its skin, so that there is a larger area over which it can absorb (take in) as much **oxygen** from the water as it needs.

Left A spatulate nosed tree frog showing off its long snout.

Below Lake Titicaca frog's loose skin drapes from its sides.

3. Long jumpers and high-fliers

The ability to suddenly jump a long distance is a good way of escaping predators. Frogs and toads have strong, long hind legs that are used for leaping on land. Some species are incredibly agile.

The American leopard frog, for example, can jump up to thirteen times its own length. Just imagine a human long jumper being able to do the same.

Tree frogs are also good leapers. They often have to jump to catch insects in flight. They have suction pads on the undersides of their feet that enable them to cling to their landing place.

Gliding tree frogs, which live in the rain forests of South America and Asia, jump the longest distances. When trying to avoid a predator they launch themselves from a tree into the air. To help them travel in the air they spread the webs of skin between the toes of their enormous hind feet. In this way they can glide long distances from tree to tree, or to the ground.

Below This gliding frog has webs of skin between its toes.

Right The back legs of the leopard frog are very long.

4. A bite to eat

Predators, such as rats and snakes, often hunt frogs and toads, but some larger species of frogs and toads may turn the tables on these enemies.

The South American horned frog, with its large mouth and sharp teeth, is a fierce predator. It regularly hunts and eats small **mammals** and snakes. In Argentina, it was believed that if a horned frog bit the lip of a grazing horse, the horse would die from the bite. This cannot be true because the horned frog does not have **poison** in its mouth, but it shows the boldness of this creature that is willing to attack animals many times its own size.

Frogs and toads will sometimes eat other frogs and toads of the same or a different species. This may seem quite shocking, but it is not surprising if you consider that frogs and toads are not fussy about what they eat. They will eat any animal that moves and is small enough to fit into their mouths.

Left The horned frog crushes its prey to death with its strong jaws.

Below A smoky jungle frog eating a puddle frog whole.

5. Disappearing acts

A good way to avoid a predator is to make sure you are difficult to see. Some species of frogs and toads rely on **camouflage** to protect them from enemies.

The European green tree frog blends into the leaves of the plants on which it lives. If it moves to a new position on a plant, it can change its color very rapidly from bright green to brown to match its new surroundings. It does this by altering the distribution of **pigments** in its skin.

The Asian leaf frog has a more permanent disguise. It lives on the forest floor and looks just like a dead leaf. Its flattened body is a golden brown color, with pointed horns over its eyes and a pointed nose. It even has ridges on its back that look like the veins of a leaf.

Below The horns of the Asian leaf frog hide its eyes from predators.

Right This European tree frog perfectly matches the leaf.

6. Warning colors

Poison arrow frogs are beautiful but deadly. Their bright colors are a warning to predators. These frogs have **glands** in their skin that contain very strong poison. The poison has a **paralyzing** effect on mammals and is strong enough to kill a small creature, such as a mouse. Poison arrow frogs live in the rain forests of South America. Local people collect the poison from the frogs' skins and smear it on the tips of their hunting arrows. They use the poison-tipped arrows to catch animals for food.

Left Predators know to avoid poison arrow frogs.

Fire-bellied toads combine camouflage with warning colors to protect themselves. The upper surfaces of their bodies are dark and blend in well with the muddy pools where they live.

In contrast, the lower surfaces of the toads' bodies are bright orange. When fire-bellied toads are threatened they throw themselves onto their backs and show their brightly colored bellies. The shock of seeing the sudden flash of color is usually enough to scare off a predator.

Below You can see why the fire-bellied toad got its name.

7. Serenading

Male frogs and toads are very noisy during the **mating season**. They gather at **breeding ponds** and sing to attract females. They make sounds using **vocal sacs** in the bottom of their mouths. The frogs breathe air into their lungs, close their mouths and nostrils, and pump air into and out of the vocal sacs to make loud noises.

The great plains toad of North America has one of the longest calls known. It can sing nonstop for several minutes. This toad has a single, large, sausage-shaped vocal sac. Frogs and toads can call continually for long periods without running out of breath because they breathe through their skins as well as with their lungs.

The varying calls of the barking tree frog tell the female where the male is and if he is ready to **mate**. The true barking call is heard only when the male is in the trees. Once he has entered the water his call changes, so the female knows that the male has entered the pond.

Below When filled with air, the vocal sac of the great plains toad is almost as big as its body.

Right The barking tree frog is so-called because its call sounds like the bark of a dog.

8.   Strange places to lay eggs

Most frogs and toads live on land as adults, but return to the water to **spawn.** You may have seen frog and toad spawn in ponds and rivers during early spring.

However, American gray tree frogs lay their eggs in trees that overhang ponds. The female makes a nest of foam from a special liquid she produces from her body. She beats the liquid up into a froth with her hind legs—and a little help from the male. The eggs are laid in the mass of foam, the outside of which soon hardens in the hot sun. **Tadpoles** hatch a few days later. They break out of the crust of the foam nest and fall into the water below.

Glass frogs of Central and South America lay their eggs on leaves that overhang water. Glass frogs are unusual because both the males and the females stay with the eggs, guarding over them and making sure they do not dry out. When the tadpoles have hatched they tumble into the water below.

Left This male glass frog is guarding the eggs.

Below These gray tree frogs are all laying eggs in the same foam nest.

9.   All change

One of the most amazing things about frogs and toads is their complete change, called **metamorphosis,** from eggs to fully grown adults.

The eggs normally hatch into tadpoles which live in water. Tadpoles look completely different from adults. They have no legs when they first hatch, they swim using their tails, and they breathe through **gills.** As they metamorphose, they gradually lose their tails and develop legs.

Adult frogs and toads will often eat tadpoles if they come across them. This does not happen often because most adults live on land and the young develop in the water. However, tadpoles of the paradoxical frog need not worry about bumping into adults. The tadpoles are three times as big as adult paradoxical frogs! Tadpoles of this species may grow to 8 inches (20 cm) long, whereas the adults are less than ½ inch.

For some species the tadpole stage takes place inside the eggs. South American rain frogs lay their eggs on leaves. The eggs contain lots of **yolk** which the tadpoles feed on as they develop. They do not emerge from the eggs until they have changed into fully formed tiny froglets.

Below The paradoxical tadpole shrinks when it becomes an adult.

Right A tiny rain froglet still encased in its egg.

10. Good fathers

In some species of frog and toad it is the male that takes on the job of caring for the eggs or young.

Male midwife toads, for example, carry the eggs around with them until they hatch. After the male and female have mated, the male winds the string of eggs around his back legs. For the next month or so he carries the eggs around with him. He spends the daylight hours secreted away in a dark, damp place, and emerges at night to feed and dampen the eggs in dew or in a pond. When the tadpoles are ready to hatch, the male takes them down to a suitable pond and allows them to swim away.

In the case of the Darwin's frog from South America, the female lays the eggs on the ground and the male stays with the eggs until the tadpoles hatch. Then the male Darwin's frog swallows the young—not into his stomach, but into his vocal sacs. The tadpoles develop for two to three months inside their father's body, and emerge through his mouth as tiny, fully-formed froglets.

Left This tiny Darwin's frog has come out from the vocal sac of its father.

Below A male midwife toad carrying a string of eggs.

11. Froggy-back rides

Strawberry poison arrow frogs lay their eggs in small pools of water at the bases of bromeliad leaves. Both the male and female parents stay close to the tadpoles as they develop. If the water in the leaves looks as though it will dry up, they carry the tadpoles away on their backs to a new pool.

Marsupial frogs also carry their tadpoles around on their backs, but underneath their skins. When the marsupial frogs mate, the male (which is much smaller than the female) sits on top of the female's back. The female leans forward so that her back slopes upward from her head. She lays eggs one at a time, and the male **fertilizes** them with his **sperm.** The eggs then roll forward into a pouch on the female's back. About twenty eggs are laid in all. When they have developed into small froglets, the young emerge from the pouch to start life on their own.

Below These marsupial froglets have just been born from the pouch on their mother's back.

Right A female strawberry poison arrow frog carrying tadpoles around on her back.

24

12. Underground havens

Frogs and toads use their skins to help them breathe. Air can only pass through the skin when it is moist, so most species live in damp places. Some species, though, manage to survive in dry places.

Spadefoot toads live in hot, dry areas in North America and Europe. They stop themselves from drying out by burrowing underground. To help them dig, they have horny pads on their hind feet.

Spadefoot toads can stay in their burrows for weeks or months at a time without feeding. The only time they emerge from their burrows is at night after a rainfall.

Australian water-holding frogs also live in dry places and burrow to keep themselves from drying out. They take up so much water into their **bladders** and into spaces underneath their skins that they swell. To prevent water being lost through their skins, they cover themselves with a clear, waterproof coat. During the dry season, people dig for the frogs to drink their water.

Left A spadefoot toad emerges from its burrow after rain.

Below This water-holding frog is removing its waterproof skin.

13. A watery world

Rather than living on land, frogs and toads of some species live entirely in water.

South American Surinam toads have flattened bodies and long sensitive fingers on their front feet. They use their fingers to feel for food in the muddy waters. Any small animal they find is seized and crammed straight into their mouths.

Adult African clawed toads also spend virtually their entire lives in water. Unlike most frogs and toads, the adults have special **organs** called lateral lines. This organ, which is also found in fish, allows them to detect movements in the water. These movements might be from a small creature like an **aquatic** insect, which the frog could eat. Or they could be from a large fish that might try to eat the frog. The lateral line helps the clawed toad to find food and escape predators.

Below Surinam toads use their fingers to find food under water.

Right African clawed toads hunt for food below the surface of the water.

GLOSSARY

Agile Being able to move quickly and easily.

Amphibians A group of animals that includes frogs, toads, newts and salamanders. Most amphibians start life as tadpoles that live in water and change into adults that live mainly on land.

Aquatic Anything that grows or lives in water.

Bladder The sac in an animal's body where urine is stored before being passed out of the body.

Breeding pond The place where, after the male and female frog or toad have mated, the fertilized eggs are left.

Camouflage The colors and patterns on the body which help the animal to blend with its surroundings.

Fertilize When a male's sperm joins with a female's egg and causes it to develop into a new individual.

Gills The feather-like organs on fish and tadpoles that allow them to breathe under water.

Gland An organ in an animal's body that produces special substances, such as poison.

Lungs The organs inside an animal's body that are used for breathing air.

Mammals A group of warm-blooded animals. The females feed their young with milk produced from their own bodies.

Mate The act performed by a male and female of a species in order to produce young.

Mating season The time of year certain species of animal mate.

Metamorphosis A series of changes, especially those that take place during the development of a tadpole into an adult.

Organ A part of an animal's body that performs a particular important job; for example, the lungs breathe in air.

Oxygen The gas that most all animals need to breathe in order to live.

Paralyzing To make an animal unable to move and therefore helpless.

Pigment The coloring substance in the skin of an animal or surface of a plant.

Poison Any substance which, when swallowed or taken into the body, causes harm or kills.

Predators Animals that hunt other animals for food.

Spawn To lay eggs. The eggs of frogs and toads are also called spawn.

Species A particular kind of plant or animal.

Sperm The male sex cells which fertilize the eggs of a female.

Tadpole The young of frogs or toads. They usually hatch from eggs and live in water. Their bodies are very different from adult bodies.

Vent The slit on the bottom of a frog or toad through which waste is passed.

Vertebrate An animal with a backbone.

Vocal sac A pocket of skin at the bottom of the mouth of a frog or toad that is often used to make mating calls.

Yolk The part of an egg that provides food for the young frog to grow and develop before it hatches.

FURTHER READING

Amazing Frogs & Toads by Barry Clarke (Alfred A. Knopf, 1991)
Frog in the Pond by Jennifer Coldrey (Gareth Stevens Inc., 1987)
Discovering Frogs & Toads by Mike Linley (Franklin Watts, 1985)
Extremely Weird Frogs by Sarah Lovett (John Muir Publications, 1991)
Frog & Toad Watching by David Webster (Julian Messner, 1986)

Picture Acknowledgments

All pictures in this book were provided by Oxford Scientific Films Ltd: G I Bernard 13, S C Bisserot 20, S Dalton 9, M Fogden cover, 5, 11, 12, 16, 18, 19, 21, 22, 24, 25, J Frazier 27, Z Leszczynski 4, 6, 7, 8, 10, 14, 15, 17, 26, 29, M Linley 23, A Ramage 28.

INDEX

Numbers in **bold** indicate photographs.